I0171549

Joseph's Journey
Volume 1

Poetry of
Hope, Help, Healing
and Humor

by

Joseph Fram

Everlasting Publishing
Yakima, Washington, USA

Joseph's Journey
Volume 1

Poetry of
Hope, Help, Healing
and Humor

by
Joseph Fram

Library of Congress Control Number:
2006922297

ISBN 0-9778083-0-0

First Edition
Everlasting Publishing
P.O. Box 1061
Yakima, WA 98907

Poetry by Joseph Fram
Compiled by his daughter,

Dana Fram Pride

*This book is dedicated to everyone
who needs hope or help or healing
with humor; or all of the above.*

My dad, one of the greatest men who has ever lived, has been a pillar of strength and source of encouragement all of my life. When he struggled through medical and personal problems, he turned to God to renew his strength and to be encouraged to reach for higher goals. Today Dad is a living miracle of how God can restore a man to health to make him able to support and give hope to others in their times of need. Everyone should have a dad who is as wonderful as my dad.

Love,
Dana

JOSEPH'S JOURNEY

A POEM IN EVERY MEMORY
by
Joseph Fram

MY EVERY MEMORY IS A POEM
BUT THEY GO BY SO FAST
IF NOT CAPTURED RIGHT AWAY
I KNOW THAT THEY WON'T LAST

SOME MEMORIES MAKE ME CHUCKLE
BUT OTHERS ARE QUITE SAD
EITHER WAY THEY COME TO ME
NONE ARE REALLY ALL THAT BAD

THEY SAY WE ALL ARE POETS
LIFE'S STAGE HAS MANY PARTS
YOU WILL SURELY HEAR YOUR POEM
IF YOU ONLY OPEN UP YOUR HEART

YES, I TOUCH EACH MEMORY
WITH CAREFUL WORDS I USE
TO MAKE EACH MEMORY DEAR TO ME
AND NOT A SINGLE ONE TO LOSE

A POEM IN EVERY MEMORY
ALL CLEARLY DO I SEE
NEVER WILL THEY CHANGE THE WORLD
SO I WRITE THESE POEMS FOR ME

BROKEN HEARTS AND LOVE
by
Joseph Fram

I SEEMS THAT WHEN TWO MARRY
TOGETHER THEY SHOULD SPEND THEIR LIFE
FOR ISN'T THAT THE DEFINITION
OF A HUSBAND AND A WIFE?

ONCE THE VOWS ARE TAKEN
DO THEY LEAVE LOVE AT THE DOOR
WHEN THEY SAY THAT PEOPLE CHANGE
WHAT'S THE USE OF LOVE FOREVERMORE

OR IS THE GAME WE PLAY NOW
TO CATCH A WOMAN OR A MAN
THEN TO MOVE TO SOMEONE ELSE
JUST BECAUSE WE CAN

MANY PEOPLE SEEM TO THINK
THAT FEELINGS PLAY NO PART
AND I GUESS THAT MAY BE TRUE
IF ONE HAS NEVER HAD A BROKEN HEART

THOUGH BROKEN HEARTS ARE FRAGILE
IN TIME THEY SURELY MEND
AND THOSE WHO STILL BELIEVE IN LOVE
ARE MUCH BETTER IN THE END

EYES OF GOD
by
Joseph Fram

I LOOKED INTO THE EYES OF GOD
WHEN I RAISED MY HEAD TO PRAY
I ASKED DIRECTIONS FOR MY LIFE
AND FOR WHAT HE HAD TO SAY

A GENTLE SMILE CAME ACROSS HIS FACE
THEN HE TOOK ME BY THE HAND
HE WHISPERED SOFTLY IN MY EAR
I CAN ONLY HELP YOU UNDERSTAND

WHEN LONG AGO I GAVE YOU LIFE
MY INTENT WAS THAT YOU HAVE FREE WILL
ALL THE CHOICES THAT YOU MAKE
ARE YOURS ALONE AND STILL

THE ONLY THING I EVER ASKED
IS TO SPREAD MY WORD OF LOVE
IF YOU DO IT ON YOUR OWN
YOU HAVE MY BLESSINGS FROM ABOVE

THEN HIS EYES LOOKED BACK AT ME
HE SAID, I'VE NO POWER OVER YOU
I CAN'T CHANGE YOUR LIFE, MY FRIEND
THAT IS SOMETHING ONLY YOU CAN DO

LOVE IS JUST MY NATURE
by
Joseph Fram

I GUESS LOVE IS JUST MY NATURE
FOR ALL MY WHOLE LIFE THROUGH
AND WHEN I TRIED ANOTHER WAY
MY MIND KNEW NOT WHAT TO DO

NOW AS I RECALL MY LIFE
ONCE, I SET MYSELF APART
NO ONE BOTHERED ME ALONE
ALONE I HAD A HEAVY HEART

WHEN SOMEONE WOULD HURT ME
I MIGHT NOT LIKE THEM FOR AWHILE
BUT IT DOESN'T LAST FOR LONG
THEN I GREET THEM WITH A SMILE

WHEN THE WORLD IS TROUBLED
BY WARS AND WICKEDNESS TO MAN
I DO NOT JOIN THE HATRED
I SPREAD LOVE WHERE E'ER I CAN

SO I GUESS IT'S JUST MY NATURE
TO SPREAD LOVE TO ALL I SEE
AND I'LL BET IF YOU LOOK AROUND
THERE ARE A LOT OF FOLKS LIKE ME

MISGUIDED

by
Joseph Fram

IF JESUS WALKED THIS EARTH TODAY
HE WOULD HIDE HIS FACE IN SHAME
FOR OUR SINS AGAINST EACH OTHER
THAT ARE TAKEN IN HIS NAME

THERE ARE THOSE WHO READ THE BIBLE
TALK OF GOD AND ALL HIS WRATH
THEY IGNORE THAT JESUS' LOVE
NEVER PREACHED A RUINOUS PATH

FOR ALL HE EVER TOLD US
TO GIVE LOVE AS YOU LOVE ME
AS FOR THOSE NOT UNDERSTANDING
HE SAID "JUST YOU LET THEM BE"

YOU WILL BE MY CHOSEN ONES
I WILL JUDGE ALL OF THE REST
YOU NEED NOT HURT AND PUNISH THEM
NOR PUT THEM TO A WORLDLY TEST

AND FOR THOSE WHO USE THE BIBLE
TO PREACH TO US THAT WE ARE WRONG
THEY IGNORE THAT JESUS LOVES US
THEY HAVE BEEN MISLED FOR SO LONG

YOU'D BE LIKE HER

by

Joseph Fram

THERE IN A CHURCH I KNELT TO PRAY
THAT I MIGHT KNOW ANOTHER'S HEART
I SOUGHT GUIDANCE FROM ABOVE
A TASK LIKE THIS, THERE IS NO START

I HAD BEEN ONCE DEEP IN LOVE
AND I THOUGHT SHE LOVED ME TOO
FOR YEARS I'D KEPT THE LOVE FOR HER
BUT YEARS BEFORE HER LOVE WAS THROUGH

THOUGH SHE STAYED SHE DID NOT SPEAK
SHE LET ME THINK HER LOVE WAS THERE
SHE GAVE HERSELF TO OTHER MEN
AND WHEN I KNEW, SHE DID NOT CARE

SHE DOES NOT SHOULDER ANY BLAME
THOUGH SHE BETRAYED HER ONE TRUE FRIEND
NOW SHE WONDERS WHY I LEFT
AND DID NOT STAY UNTIL THE END

I PRAYED TO GOD TO UNDERSTAND
HOW SHE COULD DO THIS THING TO ME
HE SOFTY SAID "YOU DON'T WANT TO KNOW
FOR THEN YOU'D BE LIKE HER, YOU SEE"

MISS THOSE TIMES
by
Joseph Fram

I FOUND A FAMILY
I THOUGHT LOST
APART FOR YEARS
AT PAINFUL COST

THE OFFSPRING OF
MY SISTER DEAR
WHOM I LOVED
AND STILL HOLD NEAR

OH, HOW PROUD
I KNOW SHE'D BE
TO SAY THIS
IS MY FAMILY

I ALSO SHARE
THIS SENSE OF PRIDE
FOR I FELT LOVE
ONCE BY THEIR SIDE

AND WHEN I FELT
HOW MUCH THEY CARE
I MISS THE TIMES
WE DIDN'T SHARE

BIRDS

by
Joseph Fram

HAVE YOU EVER WATCHED A BIRD IN FLIGHT
LOOKING FOR ITS MATE
BUSY LOOKING EVERYWHERE
HOPING THEY'RE NOT LATE

THEN THEY MEET SOME OTHER BIRDS
AND STOP TO CHAT AWHILE
HOW ARE YOU AND ALL YOUR KIDS
THEY SEEM TO ASK AND SMILE

OH, WE SEE SOME MORE GOOD FRIENDS
LET'S FIND A PLACE TO MEET
HOW ABOUT THAT WIRE OUT THERE
WHERE PHONE CALLS TICKLE LITTLE FEET

NOW LET'S SEE, HERE COME SOME MORE
LET'S STRETCH FROM END TO END
IF WE GET ENOUGH OF US
WE CAN MAKE THIS WIRE BEND

GEE, I GUESS IT'S TIME TO GO
OUR SMALL ONES MUST BE FED
TOMORROW WE TEACH THEM HOW TO FLY
SO AS NOT TO FALL OUT OF THEIR BED

MY ROAD
by
Joseph Fram

I HAVE WALKED MY ROAD OF LIFE
AND WHERE EACH BEND TURNED
ANOTHER SIDE OF LIFE I SAW
ANOTHER LESSON I HAVE LEARNED

AT THE START I HAD BEEN TOLD
THE ROAD WAS STRAIGHT AND NARROW
HAD MY ROAD NOT HAD A BEND
ALL BIRDS WOULD BE A SPARROW

THOUGH THE ROAD HAD MANY BENDS
THERE WERE BORDERS I DEFINED
WHEN TEMPTATION BECKONED ME
I SAW THEM IN MY MIND

OTHERS SOMETIMES SHARED MY ROAD
IN SEARCH OF ONE THEIR OWN
WHEN OUR SHARING WAS COMPLETE
I WOULD WALK MY ROAD ALONE

HOW MANY BENDS, HOW SHORT THE STRAIGHT
IS SOMETHING I DON'T KNOW
I ONLY KNOW THIS ROAD IS MINE
THE ONLY ROAD I'LL EVER GO

CHRISTLIKE CHRISTMAS

by
Joseph Fram

AND NOW AT CHRISTMAS TIME
I CONTEMPLATE MY YEAR
I ASK IF IT WAS CHRISTLIKE
NOT KNOWING WHAT I'LL HEAR

HAVE I FORGIVEN TRESPASSERS
AND ASKED OF OTHERS FOR THE SAME
HAVE I PRACTICED BEING CHRISTLIKE
OR AM I CHRISTIAN JUST IN NAME

I SOMETIMES GOT BAD FEELINGS
INSIDE THEY WERE QUITE STRONG
DID THEY DO MY SOUL SOME DAMAGE
BY HOLDING ON TO THEM TOO LONG

IT IS LOVE THAT JESUS TAUGHT US
HE AWAITS WE HEAR THE CALL
AND HAVE LOVE FOR ONE ANOTHER
THE GREATEST CHRISTMAS GIFT OF ALL

TIS THE SEASON TO BE CHRISTLIKE
LET IT CARRY ON NEXT YEAR
TO FACE THOSE TRIALS AND TRIBULATIONS
AND WALK IN LIGHT AND HAVE NO FEAR

NEVER A FRIEND
by
Joseph Fram

I HAD FALLEN AND YOU LEFT ME
I WAS WEAK AND REACHED FOR YOU
WHEN YOU OFFERED NOT YOUR HAND
I THOUGHT THEN THAT I WAS THROUGH

WE HAD COME A LONG, LONG WAY
I REACHED WHEN YOU WERE DOWN
I OFFERED YOU MY HELPING HAND
IN YOUR NEED I WAS AROUND

YOU HAD ALWAYS CALLED ME FRIEND
TO ME, IT MEANT I'D COUNT ON YOU
WE WOULD HOLD EACH OTHER UP
THEN, AND FOR OUR LIFETIME TOO

THEN WE CROSSED LIFE'S DESERT
THE ONLY TIME I'D NEED A HAND
WHEN I ASKED YOU SHADE MY EYES
YOU LEFT ME LYING IN THE SAND

THOUGH I STILL CANNOT BELIEVE IT
YOU SHOWED YOUR COLORS IN THE END
WHAT HURTS ME MORE THAN LOSING YOU
TO KNOW YOU NEVER WERE A FRIEND

LOVE IS NEVER OLD
by
Joseph Fram

ANOTHER YEAR TO SHOUT ABOUT
NOW THAT YOU ARE SIXTY-FIVE
EYES SO BRIGHT AND SPRINGY STEP
AREN'T YOU GLAD THAT YOU'RE ALIVE

WHEN I THINK OF ALL WE'VE DONE
I FEEL JUST LIKE A TEEN
I JUST REGRET SOME YOUTH WAS LOST
WE WEREN'T TOGETHER IN BETWEEN

TOGETHER WE HAVE SEEN THE WORLD
BUT THERE IS MORE FOR US TO SEE
I KNOW THIS AGE IS SURELY GOLD
I HOPE FOR YOU, IT IS FOR ME

THOSE WHO SAY WE'RE GROWING OLD
SPEAK WITH A FORKED TONGUE
FOR WITH EACH NEW PASSING YEAR
I REALLY THINK WE'RE GROWING YOUNG

AS YOU GROW EACH PASSING YEAR
YOU GROW FONDER IN MY HEART
IN THIS POEM MY BIRTHDAY GIFT
MY LOVE TILL DEATH DO US PART

NEVER ALONE

by

Joseph Fram

GOD GIVE US LIFE
TO BE ON EARTH A WHILE
TILL HE CALLS US HOME
TO SHARE HIS ETERNAL SMILE

FOR THOSE HE LEAVES BEHIND
THEIR WORK IS NOT YET DONE
HE WAITS IN HIS HOUSE
WITH ROOM FOR EVERYONE

ONE AT A TIME
HE WILL CALL US HOME
AND LEAVE ENOUGH BEHIND
SO WE ARE NEVER ALONE

BROKEN HEARTS

by
Joseph Fram

ONCE A HEART IS BROKEN
THEY SAY IT NEVER MENDS
AND FOR BROKEN HEARTED LOVERS
ARE THEY ONLY NOW JUST FRIENDS

BROKEN HEARTS STAY BROKEN
WHEN THE FIRST REAL LOVE IS LOST
DO OTHER LOVES THAT TRY TO MEND
HAVE TO PAY THE COST

BROKEN HEARTS ARE TENDER
THEY SEARCH UNTIL THEY FIND
ANOTHER BROKEN HEART THAT NEEDS THEM
TO BE GENTLE, TRUE AND KIND

BROKEN HEARTS THAT GET TOGETHER
PROTECT EACH OTHER FROM THE PAIN
AND REALIZE TWICE BROKEN HEARTS
MAY NOT SURVIVE AGAIN

IF BROKEN HEARTS CAN NEVER MEND
BUT WE PICK UP ALL THE PARTS
WHEN WE MEET OUR JUDGMENT DAY
IS THERE A PLACE FOR BROKEN HEARTS

A MESSAGE TO MAX
by
Joseph Fram

GOD HAS SEEN YOUR WORK ON EARTH
YOU'VE DONE EVERYTHING HE PLANNED
NOW HE WANTS YOU IN HIS HOUSE
HE SENDS THIS MESSAGE BY MY HAND

THE SCENES THAT I HAVE PUT ON EARTH
YOU PAINTED FOR ALL TO SEE
NOW HEAVEN ALSO HAS SOME SCENES
THAT YOU WILL PAINT FOR ME

NOT EVERYONE CAN COME WITH ME
I CHOOSE THOSE WHICH ARE THE BEST
THERE IS NO DEATH WITHIN MY HOUSE
I ONLY LAY YOU DOWN TO REST

THROUGH ALL THE TRIALS WHILE ON EARTH
YOU SERVED ME WELL UNTIL THE END
BECAUSE OF THIS, YOU ARE WITH ME
YOU'RE IN MY HOUSE, MY FRIEND

JUST LOOK AROUND AND YOU WILL SEE
YOU ARE WITH THOSE THAT YOU LOVE
FOR ALL OF THOSE YOU LEFT BEHIND
WE WILL WAIT FROM UP ABOVE

OH! SO NICE
by
Joseph Fram

IT IS OH! SO NICE TO HAVE YOU
SO EVER CLOSE TO ME
I HAVE SEARCHED FOR ALL MY LIFE
THIS IS WHERE I WANT TO BE

WE UNDERSTAND EACH OTHER
DO THE THINGS WE LIKE TO DO
IF WE FIND SOME OTHER THINGS
WE MOSTLY TRY THEM TOO

WE KEEP OUR LIVES REAL SIMPLE
LOVE IS ALL WE HAVE TO UNDERSTAND
AND CONFUSION TURNS TO PEACE
WHEN WE HOLD EACH OTHER'S HAND

WE'VE BEEN TOGETHER LONG ENOUGH
TO PROVE THAT I WAS RIGHT
TO PICK SOMEONE FROM '32
WHEN WE MET BY CHANCE THAT NIGHT

HAPPY BIRTHDAY ALL AGAIN
I'M GLAD THAT WE'RE TOGETHER
IN AGE, IN LOVE AND ALL THE THINGS
TO TAKE US THROUGH ALL WEATHER

ROSES

by
Joseph Fram

THERE ARE ROSES IN MY LIFE
THAT I STOPPED TO SMELL
OTHERS THAT I WISHED I HAD
THOSE I KNOW TOO WELL

THERE WERE ROSES THAT I PICKED
THAT NEVER WON AN EARTHLY PRIZE
GOD JUST LED ME TO THEIR BED
"I GREW THEM FOR YOUR EYES"

MANY TIMES I PICKED A ROSE
ONLY TO HAVE THE PETALS FALL
WHY I DIDN'T NURTURE THEM
I LOOK BACK AND CAN'T RECALL

OTHERS THAT I CHERISHED SO
I CRUSHED THEM IN A BOOK
ALL THEIR BEAUTY IS STILL THERE
EACH TIME I TAKE ANOTHER LOOK

OF ALL THE ROSES THAT I PICKED
I'D NOT RETURN A SINGLE ONE
EACH OF THEM WAS DEAR TO ME
THERE'S NO REGRET IN WHAT I'VE DONE

CHRISTMAS CANDLE

By
Joseph Fram

WELL, WELL, WELL
WHAT HAVE WE HERE
IT'S CHRISTMAS TIME
FOR ONE MORE YEAR

THE YEAR WENT SO FAST
I MOST NEAR LOST TRACK
GOOD FRIENDS AND MEMORIES
I WOULDN'T TAKE BACK

THE CHRISTMAS WISH
I MADE LAST YEAR
HAS BEEN FULFILLED
I AM STILL HERE

SO FILL MY STOCKING
WITH LOVE AND FRIENDS
AND ONE CAN TRAVEL
WHERE ERE THE ROAD BENDS

MERRY CHRISTMAS TO ALL
AND PEACE IN EACH HEART
ONE CANDLE IN DARKNESS
IS A GOOD PLACE TO START

FATHER'S LOVE
by
Joseph Fram

WHEN I THINK OF DAUGHTERS
GOD COULD HAVE GIVEN ME
HE KNEW THAT IF IT WERE YOU
I'D BE AS HAPPY AS CAN BE

I NEVER HAD A QUESTION
ABOUT ANYTHING HE'D DONE
EVERY DAY I THANK HIM
FOR GIVING ME THIS ONE

IN MY LIFE YOU'RE SPECIAL
I HAVE ALWAYS LOVED YOU SO
I SHOULDN'T HAVE TO TELL YOU
WHAT YOU ALREADY KNOW

A FATHER'S LOVE GOES ON AND ON
UNTIL THE END OF TIME
AND NOTHING MAKES ME PROUDER
THAN TO SAY THIS DAUGHTER'S MINE

FOR NOW AND FOREVER

by
Joseph Fram

FOR NOW AND FOREVER
TWO HEARTS BEAT AS ONE
AND UPON EACH MORNING'S WAKE
A NEW WORLD HAS BEGUN

SO WE LEAVE THE PAST BEHIND
AND TOMORROW IS NOT HERE
WHAT IS HERE IS LOVE TODAY
THAT WE HOLD SO DEAR

THOUGH OUR LIVES ARE DIFFERENT
ON ONE THING WE CAN AGREE
THERE IS NAUGHT SO IMPORTANT
AS LOVE 'TWEEN YOU AND ME

YOU ARE WHAT I TAKE YOU
AND YOU THE SAME FOR ME
WE ARE HOW GOD MADE US
SO WHAT ELSE CAN WE BE

NO NEED TO WAIT FOREVER
FOR WHAT WE HAVE IS NOW
WE KNOW THAT LOVE IS ENDLESS
AND WILL NEVER END SOMEHOW

LITTLE BROTHER GEORGE
by
Joseph Fram

HERE'S TO MY LITTLE BROTHER
THE ONLY ONE I EVER HAD
PESTY SOMETIMES AS A CHILD
BUT NEVER REALLY ALL THAT BAD

I KNOW I ALWAYS LOVED HIM
I WAS PROUD AS I COULD BE
HE WAS GOOD IN ALL THE SPORTS
I WISHED THAT I COULD BE LIKE HE

AND THEN SOMEHOW I WENT AWAY
I LOST TOUCH AND THAT WAS SAD
THEN WHEN I SAW HIM YESTERDAY
I MISSED THE TIMES WE NEVER HAD

OUR LITTLE TIME TOGETHER NOW
HAS BECOME SO PRECIOUS UNTO ME
THOUGH LOVE SURROUNDS ME WHERE I GO
IT'S NOT THE SAME AS FAMILY

HE WILL ALWAYS BE MY LITTLE BROTHER
THOUGH HE'S OLDER NOW AND GROWN
I WISH THAT WE'D BEEN CLOSER NOW
-IF ONLY THEN THAT I HAD KNOWN-

PRAYER

by
Joseph Fram

WELL, YES I'VE SAID A PRAYER OR TWO
AND ASKED FROM THE BOTTOM OF MY HEART
ONCE OFFERING UP THESE PRAYERS TO GOD
I THOUGHT I'D DONE MY PART

THERE WERE PRAYERS FOR LITTLE THINGS
AND I GUESS SOME BIG ONES TOO
WHEN THESE PRAYERS WERE ANSWERED NOT
I KNEW NOT WHAT TO DO

I WISHED CONTROL OF LIFE WITH PRAYER
SO AS TO OBEY MY EVERY WILL
LIKE BRINGING BACK THE GOOD OL' DAYS
I COULDN'T MAKE THE TIME STAND STILL

WHEN SOMEONE ELSE WAS PRAYING TOO
TO FEEL THE SAME AS ME
I ALWAYS ASKED THE QUESTION THEN
WHICH ANSWERED PRAYER HAD COME TO BE

NOW MY PRAYER IS SIMPLE
AS EACH DAY IS BEGUN
I DO NOT ASK FOR ANYTHING
ONLY THAT THY WILL BE DONE

HEAVEN BOUND

for
Kathleen Collins
by
Joseph Fram

GOD PICKS THE TIME
TO CALL US HOME
IT MATTERS NOT
TO WHERE WE ROAM

WHEN HE TOOK OUR JIMMY
HE SAID "YOUR WORK IS DONE"
BUT TO ALL AROUND US
'TWAS THOUGHT IT JUST BEGUN

JIMMY HELPED THE NEEDY
NEVER COUNTED UP THE COST
BUT IN THE EYES OF GOD
NOT A DEED WAS EVER LOST

AND NOW ALL WILL MISS HIM
HIS FAMILY LEFT ON EARTH
BUT GOD LEAVES OTHER CHILDREN
TO REMIND US OF HIS WORTH

WE ARE ALL SADDENED
ASK THAT REASON BE FOUND
GOD WILL EXPLAIN TO US LATER
WHY JIMMY IS NOW HEAVEN BOUND

MY GOD

by
Joseph Fram

WHEN MY GOD IS SPEAKING
I CAN FEEL HIS GENTLE TOUCH
HE TELLS ME WHAT I NEED TO KNOW
IN WORDS THAT AREN'T TOO MUCH

LET KINDNESS GUIDE YOUR EVERY WORD
BE GENTLE WITH THE FRAIL
I WILL HELP YOU START AGAIN
EACH TIME I SEE YOU FAIL

I WILL ALWAYS GIVE YOU LOVE
THERE IS NO NEED FOR FEAR
YOU MUST NOT BETRAY YOURSELF
FOR THAT'S WHAT KEEPS US NEAR

ALWAYS RESPECT YOUR FELLOW MAN
JUDGE NOT AND LET HIM BE
I ALSO TOLD HIM ALL THESE THINGS
HE MUST SEEK HIS PEACE WITH ME

MY GOD IS KIND AND GENTLE
WHEN YOU LOOK, I HOPE YOU SEE
THE TIMES THAT I CAN'T WALK ALONE
IS WHEN HE CARRIES ME

SANDS OF TIME
by
Joseph Fram

AS I CHARGED ON OH SO RIGHTEOUS
ONCE SO LONG AGO
I CAN SEE NOW OH SO CLEARLY
T'WAS FRUIT OF SEEDS YOU SOW

FOR IN MY YOUTH OF PERPETUITY
ALL THE ANSWERS CAME TO ME
AND WITH EASE OF BLACK AND WHITENESS
ALL SOLUTIONS DID I SEE

IT DIDN'T BOTHER THAT SOME OTHERS
COULD NOT SHARE THE WORLD I DREW
FOR I KNEW THAT GOD HAD GRANTED ME
INSIGHT INTO HIS POINT OF VIEW

NOW AS I CAST A BACKWARD GLANCE
I SEE MY CASTLES FALL
THE SANDS OF TIME I BUILT THEM ON
HAVE NEARLY CHANGED THEM ALL

IF PERHAPS I HAD NOT ACTED
THERE WOULD BE NO CHANGE AT ALL
FOR IN LIMBO ALL WOULD STAY
WAITING FOR ANOTHER'S FUTURE CALL

A THOUGHT OF LOVE ON MOTHER'S DAY

by
Joseph Fram

WE MET AT A TIME
WITH MY LIFE IN GREAT DESPAIR
I'D BE NOT HERE TODAY
BUT FOR YOU BEING THERE

YOU LIFTED UP MY LIFE
WHEN I MOST NEEDED A HAND
AND STEADIED MY WORLD
SO I ONCE AGAIN COULD STAND

ALL DURING THIS TIME
YOU ASKED NOTHING OF ME
BUT BE TRUE TO MYSELF
AND SHARE LOVE WITH THEE

MY LOVE HAS GROWN
AS EACH DAY BECOMES PAST
THE ONE THING I NOW HAVE
IS A LOVE THAT WILL FOREVER LAST

AND NOW ON YOUR DAY
LET IT BE KNOWN
THOUGH WE EACH HAVE A FAMILY
THEY SEEM BOTH TO BE OUR OWN

SEARCHES END
by
Joseph Fram

I OPENED UP MY EYES ONE DAY
IN A WORLD FAR FROM THAT I'D KNOWN
IT WAS FILLED WITH HAPPY THINGS
I THOUGHT, 'HOW MUCH I'VE GROWN'

THERE IS LOVE AND HAPPINESS
ONE TO SHARE MY TENDER DREAMS
EVERYWHERE WE GO IS BLISS
LIFE IS REALLY WHAT IT SEEMS

HER GENTLE TOUCH, HER TENDER KISS
THE KINDNESS WHEN SHE SPEAKS TO ME
SHE GAVE ME BACK WHAT I HAD LOST
ALL SHE ASKS, WE SPEAK OF WE

SHE LEAVES EACH DAY AN OPEN DOOR
TO LET HER LOVE SHINE THROUGH
THROUGH HER LOVE I HEAR HER SAY
THERE IS NOTHING WE CAN'T DO

I LOVE THIS NEW WORLD I AM IN
WHERE TWO IN LOVE MAKE HARMONY
FOR I NO LONGER SEARCH FOR LOVE
THERE IS NO NEED INSIDE OF ME

ONLY A MAN

by

Joseph Fram

I HEARD GOD CALLING
MY NAME OUT ONE DAY
I THOUGHT HE WAS HERE
TO TAKE ME AWAY

HE LOOKED SOMEWHAT PUZZLED
AS I GOT READY TO GO
THAT'S WHEN HE TOLD ME
THERE ARE THINGS THAT YOU SHOULD KNOW

YOU LIFE IS SO PRECIOUS
YOU DON'T KNOW WHAT IT'S WORTH
AND YOU HAVE IT OH SO SHORTLY
WHILE YOU TRAVEL ON THIS EARTH

YOU DON'T SEE THAT EACH DAY
IS SO BLESSED AND SO DEAR
AND ALL RICHES THAT YOU GATHER
WHEN YOU DIE, WILL DISAPPEAR

I HAVE COME HERE TO TELL YOU
LOVE ALL THOSE THAT YOU CAN
I MAY TAKE YOU TOMORROW
FOR YOU ARE ONLY A MAN

CHRISTMAS GIFTS
by
Joseph Fram

JUST AS SURE AS CLOCKWORK
CHRISTMAS ROLLS AROUND EACH YEAR
WHEN WE EXCHANGE THOSE PRESENTS
WE GIVE AND GET FROM SOMEONE DEAR

WE HOPE THAT ALL THE THINGS WE WANT
ARE HIDDEN SOMEWHERE 'NEATH THE TREE
AND HOPE THAT REALLY PRETTY ONE
WAS PUT THERE JUST FOR ME

IT HAS TAKEN WEEKS OF PREPARATION
TO ASSURE EVERYTHING IS RIGHT
WE HOPE NO ONE IS DISAPPOINTED
WITH THEIR PRESENTS CHRISTMAS NIGHT

I HOPE ONE GIFT IS NOT FORGOTTEN
AS IT WAS MEANT FOR EVERYONE
AND THAT'S THE CHRIST CHILD JESUS
A GIFT FROM GOD -- HIS ONLY SON

AND SO A MERRY CHRISTMAS
AND A MERRY SONG
AND ON MY CHRISTMAS WISH LIST
MERRY CHRISTMAS ALL YEAR LONG

THANK YOU, ENGLAND

by
Joseph Fram

I HAD ME SOME FISH AND CHIPS
AND AT CRICKET HAD A GO
THERE WERE PLENTY CHAPS AROUND ME
DOING WHAT, I DO NOT KNOW

THE WOMEN THERE WERE CHARMING
BUT SOMEHOW LOOKED THE SAME
I COULDN'T BRING MYSELF TO ASK
IF THEY SHARED A COMMON NAME

ALL THE FOOD WAS OH SO GOOD
A TRICK THEY PLAYED UPON THEIR SWEETS
FOR NO MATTER WHAT YOU HAD
THE TASTE WAS LIKE ALL THE OTHER EATS

I REALLY HAD A GRAND OL' TIME
AS I WOULD WALK AROUND
I LISTENED AS THEY SPOKE TO ME
TO TRY TO RECOGNIZE SOME SOUND

AND NOW I THANK YOU, ENGLAND
FOR ALL YOU'VE SHOWN TO ME
NOW THAT I AM HOME AGAIN
IT'S NOT THAT BAD A PLACE TO BE

TO RELIVE AGAIN
by
Joseph Fram

OUR LIVES ARE SPENT
FROM DAY TO DAY
WITH NAUGHT WRIT DOWN
BUT MUCH TO SAY

THERE ARE THOSE MOMENTS
THAT TOUCH US ALL
WHEN WE'RE CAST DOWN
OR STANDING TALL

AND AT THAT TIME
WE CLEARLY SEE
THAT WHAT WE ARE
OR PERHAPS SHOULD BE

THE MOMENT'S LOST
LEST WE SEIZE IT NOW
PRECIOUS MEMORIES SEEP
THROUGH OUR GRASP SOMEHOW

AND SO I TAKE
EVERY NOW AND THEN
A THOUGHT TO VERSE
TO RELIVE AGAIN

TROUBLES

by

Joseph Fram

I HAVE GIVEN THOUGHT TO TROUBLES
AND THE WAY THEY COME AROUND
IT IS ALWAYS LEAST EXPECTED
WHEN SURELY THEY ARE FOUND

MOSTLY THEY ARE SMALL ONES
BUT BIG ONES THERE ARE TOO
THE PROBLEM THAT THEY POSE IS
THEY NEVER COME AS FEW

AND WHEN I HAVE SOME TROUBLES
IN ORDER DO THEY GO
SOMETIMES I'LL WORK THE BIG ONES
AND HOLD THE SMALL ONES SO

IF I NEED SOME HELP
UPON A FRIEND I'LL CALL
USUALLY AS IT WINDS UP
I WISH I HADN'T CALLED AT ALL

I COME UP WITH SOLUTIONS
AND I KNOW JUST WHAT TO DO
THE ONLY PROBLEM FOLLOWS
LOSE ONE AND PICK UP TWO

VALENTINE LOVE

by
Joseph Fram

IF MY HEART HAD ONLY KNOWN
THAT SOMEDAY YOU'D BE WITH ME
IT WOULD NEVER HAD TO SUFFER
AND TO SEE THINGS IT'D SEE

FOR IT COULD BEAR THE WAITING
AND ENDURE WHATEVER PAIN
IT WOULD SMILE THROUGH THE SORROW
KNOWING LOVE WOULD COME AGAIN

SOMETIMES THE THINGS WE DO
CAN SEPARATE US FROM THE HEART
BUT IN THE END THERE'S WINNING
WHEN NEW DAYS BRINGS LOVE'S NEW START

NOW MY HEART HAS FOUND YOU
IT WILL NEVER LET YOU GO
BUT IF IT HAD ONLY KNOWN THEN
IT WOULD HAVE SOUGHT YOU LONG AGO

SO PLEASE ACCEPT THIS VALENTINE
WITH IT ALL MY HEARTFELT LOVE
CARRY IT HERE ON EARTH
AND TILL WE MEET ABOVE

WHAT?

by
Joseph Fram

I USED TO REMEMBER
ALL THINGS THAT WERE SAID
ALL NUMBERS AND PICTURES
AND THINGS THAT I READ

IT USED TO BE EASY
WITH AN ANSWER SO SLICK
AND EVERYTHING DONE
IT USED TO BE QUICK

I USED TO GET CALLS
FROM THOSE ALL AROUND
WHATEVER THE ANSWER
IT'D ALWAYS BE FOUND

THEN SOMETHING HAPPENED
I GUESS I GOT OLD
NOW EVERY QUESTION
I JUST PUT ON HOLD

WHAT WAS SO IMPORTANT
I WAS JUST GOING TO SAY
WAS ON THE TIP OF MY TONGUE
THEN IT JUST SLIPPED AWAY

CHRISTMAS JINGLE
by
Joseph Fram

JINGLE BELLS -- JINGLE BELLS
WHAT DID I FORGET
GOT ALL THE CHILDREN'S PRESENTS
EVEN GOT ONE FOR THE PET

CHRISTMAS SONGS ARE RINGING
ALL DAY THROUGH MY HEAD
RIGHT FROM THANKSGIVING MORNING
UNTIL MY NEW YEAR'S BED

IT'S NICE TO HAVE A CHRISTMAS
THAT REALLY LASTS SO LONG
AND TO TOP THAT CHRISTMAS FEELING
WITH A GOOD OLD CHRISTMAS SONG

I'D LIKE TO KEEP THE CHRISTMAS SPIRIT
WITH ME THROUGHOUT THE YEAR
AND SHARE THE LOVE OF CHRISTMAS
WITH ALL AND HAVE NO FEAR

JINGLE BELLS -- JINGLE BELLS
DON'T FORGET ON CHRISTMAS MORN
THE REASON WE HAVE CHRISTMAS
IS BECAUSE OUR CHRIST WAS BORN

THE ONE I AM

by

Joseph Fram

I CAN NOT BE ANOTHER ONE
NOR DO THE THINGS THAT OTHERS DO
WHAT GOD HAS GIVEN ME IS MINE
AND TO THAT IMAGE I'LL BE TRUE

WHEN I HEAR OF HEROIC DEEDS
SOMETIMES I WISH THAT IT WERE ME
BUT THEN AGAIN I'D LOSE MYSELF
I WOULDN'T KNOW THEN WHO I'D BE

IF ALL THE WEALTH I WANT WERE MINE
WOULD I BE HAPPIER THEN THAN NOW
COULD I REARRANGE THE WORLD
OR EVEN THAT I WOULD KNOW HOW

WOULD I THEN BECOME A GUARD
AND HORDE MY PRIZES TO THE END
WOULD NO ONE WEEP WHEN I PASSED ON
CAUSE I FORGOT TO MAKE A FRIEND

OR PERHAPS THE ONE I AM
INSPIRES SOME TO STOP AND STARE
IN THEIR MIND, MAYBE THEY SAY
I ONLY WISH THAT I WERE THERE

THE OLD SCHOOL
by
Joseph Fram

NORMAN ROCKWELL CAME TO MIND
AT SCENES LOST FOR MANY YEARS
IT TURNED PAGES IN MY MIND
AND THE LONGING BROUGHT SOME TEARS

IT WAS SUCH A SIMPLE SCENE
AN UNFENCED FIELD WITH TINY STAND
WHERE THERE ONCE WERE FOOTBALLS GAMES
AND THOSE WHO PLAYED KNEW IT WAS GRAND

CLOSE BEHIND A SCHOOLHOUSE STOOD
WHERE THE BIBLE STILL WAS TAUGHT
AND CLASSROOM PICTURES SMILED AT ME
THAT THOSE STILL ALIVE HAVE NOT FORGOT

THEN I SAW A DESK OR TWO
INITIALS CARVED UPON THEIR SIDE
WITH A SIMPLE "I LOVE YOU"
NOT TRYING VERY HARD TO HIDE

WHEN I RECALL THE FUN I HAD
AT A SCHOOL THAT COULD BE THIS
MY HEART WEEPS FOR CHILDREN NOW
BECAUSE I KNOW WHAT THEY WILL MISS

WHAT'S LEFT IS LOVE
by
Joseph Fram

SOME FIFTY YEARS
OF TIME HAS PASSED
YOU RAISED YOUR KIDS
NO EASY TASK

YES THERE ARE TIMES
BOTH GOOD AND BAD
A TIME FOR LAUGHTER
A TIME FOR SAD

THE WORK WAS HARD
WITH SOME COMPLAINTS
YOU'RE STILL TOGETHER
YOU MUST BE SAINTS

AND THROUGH IT ALL
YOU BOTH STOOD TALL
TO KEEP A MARRIAGE
THAT WOULD NOT FALL

SO HAND IN HAND
HELP FROM ABOVE
ALL FILTERED OUT
WHAT'S LEFT IS LOVE

WHEEL

by
Joseph Fram

I SEE EVERYTHING IN POETRY
AND NOT IN BLACK AND WHITE
SOMEHOW ALL THE POEMS I MAKE
IN MY MIND ARE ALWAYS RIGHT

I WASN'T ALWAYS THIS ROMANTIC
I THOUGHT POETS LIVED ALONE
I DID WHAT ALL AROUND ME SAID
AND ONLY TURNED THE OL' GRINDSTONE

THEN ONE DAY I LEFT THAT WHEEL
I THOUGHT FOR JUST A WHILE
BUT POEMS DANCED WITHIN MY HEAD
SOME BROUGHT ME TEARS AND SOME A SMILE

I THOUGHT I COULDN'T LEAVE THAT WHEEL
I THOUGHT MY WORLD WOULD FALL APART
IT WASN'T TILL I LEFT THAT WHEEL
I BEGAN FEELING WITH MY HEART

YOUR HEART WILL TAKE YOU EVERYWHERE
BUT WITH A POEM OR WITH A SONG
NOW WHEN I LOOK AT THAT COLD WHEEL
I JUST WONDER HOW I GOT ALONG

WHEN A CHILD DIES
by
Joseph Fram

IT SEEMS WHEN PARENTS ARE PRECEDED
BY THEIR CHILD WHEN IT DIES
THERE IS THE AWFUL TASK OF WONDERING
AND ASKING ALL THE WHYS

WE WON'T KNOW ALL THE ANSWERS
BUT GOD GAVE US A WINDOW WE COULD SEE
FOR THEY WILL ALWAYS BE WITH US
IN WHAT WE CALL OUR MEMORY

IN OUR MEMORY'S WINDOW
WE CAN SEE THAT CHILD AT PLAY
AND ALL OF THOSE FUN THINGS
WE DID ON SPECIAL HOLIDAY

WE SEE THAT CHILD GROWING
AND HAD SO MUCH MORE TO LEARN
AND WE CAN STILL REMEMBER
HOW THEY ANXIOUSLY AWAIT THEIR TURN

THEN WE SEE THEM ALL GROWN UP
HOW COULD IT HAPPEN OH THAT FAST
JUST YESTERDAY THEY WERE CHILDREN
THOSE ARE THE MEMORIES THAT WILL LAST

FOR NOW THEY ARE IN HEAVEN
GOD HAD THAT IN HIS PLAN
AND FOR THOSE OF US HE LEFT BEHIND
HE WILL DO ALL THAT HE CAN

UNKEPT HEARTACHE

by
Joseph Fram

I DIDN'T KEEP THAT HEARTACHE
YOU LEFT WHEN YOU WENT AWAY
I GUESS YOU DIDN'T REALLY CARE
IF IT WOULD GO OR IT WOULD STAY

HEARTACHES CAN SURELY HINDER
AND THEY REALLY ARE NOT FUN
FOR EVERY TIME YOU THINK IT'S OVER
YOU KNOW IT'S JUST BEGUN

THEY WILL MAKE YOU DO DUMB THINGS
SAY THINGS THAT YOU'D NEVER SAY
THEY WON'T LET YOU SLEEP AT NIGHT
AND HAUNT YOU ALL THE DAY

BUT HEARTACHES HAVE A PLACE IN LIFE
IF ONE DECIDES TO LOVE ANEW
FOR LOVE IS SO MUCH STRONGER THEN
IF YOUR NEW LOVE'S HAD ONE TOO

I DIDN'T KEEP THAT HEARTACHE
THERE IS TOO MUCH LIFE TO LIVE
AND TOO MUCH LOVE WITHIN MY HEART
TO HOLD INSIDE AND NEVER GIVE

41

WHEN LOVE IS TRUE
by
Joseph Fram

THERE IS NO DEATH WHEN LOVE IS TRUE
JUST LIFE ON EARTH IS O'ER
FOR LOVE ITSELF IS THERE TO LAST
FROM TIME BEGAN AND MORE

FOR THOSE WHO FIND A LOVE THAT'S TRUE
THEIR SOULS WILL NEVER PART
AND THOUGH THOSE SOULS HAVE ALWAYS BEEN
IT'S HERE ON EARTH THEY GET A HEART

SURELY SOULS HAVE MET BEFORE
EACH ONE SEARCHING FOR ITS MATE
SOMETIMES THEY'RE NOT FOUND ON EARTH
THOUGH THEY'RE NOT, IT IS NOT TOO LATE

FOR A SOUL WILL NEVER REST
TILL THAT SOMEONE COMES ALONG
AND ONE MAY LIVE A LIFE OR TWO
TRUE LOVE WON'T PERMIT IT WRONG

AND SO FOR EACH THERE IS A MATE
WHEN TIME STANDS STILL AND WAITS FOR YOU
AND THAT LOVE WILL ALWAYS BE
THERE IS NO DEATH WHEN LOVE IS TRUE

WHY?

by
Joseph Fram

JESUS GAVE HIS KEYS TO PETER
HIS WORK TO CARRY ON
ASKING ONLY LOVE FOR ALL
TO CONTINUE WHEN HE'S GONE

JUST REMEMBER WHAT I TAUGHT YOU
WHEN IN THE TEMPLE BOTH WE STOOD
A TEMPLE IS FOR WORSHIP
NOT FOR MONEYCHANGERS' GOOD

I ASK THAT YOU CONSIDER
THE NEEDS OF EVERY LESSER MAN
REGARDLESS YOUR POSSESSIONS
GIVE HIM EVERYTHING YOU CAN

IF YOU THINK YOU NEED A TEMPLE
DO NOT BUILD IT IN MY NAME
YOU KNOW PRAYING IN A CLOSET
I WILL HEAR YOU JUST THE SAME

WHEN I SEE THESE TEMPLES
BUILT HALF WAY TO THE SKY
I DO NOT THINK OF WORSHIP
IT ONLY MAKES ME WONDER WHY

THEN IT WAS CHRISTMAS
by
Joseph Fram

IT WAS EARLY THIS YEAR
WHEN MY FIRST PRESENT CAME
IT WAS SO OVERWHELMING
AND YET WITHOUT NAME

I WILL NEVER FORGET
HOW GOD LED ME TO SEE
A GIFT OF TOMORROW
WOULD BE GIVEN TO ME

I WAS GIVEN GREAT RICHES
BUT NOT OF THIS EARTH
TO GREET EACH NEW DAY
HOW CAN I MEASURE ITS WORTH

NOW ALL IN THANKSGIVING
I PRAY OTHERS WILL SEE
IT NEED NOT BE DECEMBER
FOR IT CHRISTMAS TO BE

FOR CHRISTMAS IS GIVING
AND GIVING WITH LOVE
EACH DAY SHOULD BE CHRISTMAS
A GIFT FROM ABOVE

WHEN A SOUL IS HEAVY
by
Joseph Fram

WHEN A SOUL IS HEAVY
NO ONE ELSE CAN REALLY SEE
ALL THE TORMENT AND THE ANGUISH
AND HOW ALONE THAT SOUL CAN BE

THERE IS NO CONSOLATION
FROM FRIENDS THAT WISH IT WELL
FOR THEY WILL NEVER UNDERSTAND
WHAT IT'S LIKE TO LIVE IN HELL

OH, THAT SOUL WILL GO ALONG
AND PRETEND THERE IS NO STRIFE
BUT THERE WILL NEVER BE A DOUBT
THAT THE WEIGHT WILL LAST FOR LIFE

WHEN ONE IS HURT UNTO THEIR SOUL
THE TEARS INSIDE WILL ALWAYS FLOW
THEY WILL NEVER BE RELEASED
THEY HAVE NO WHERE ELSE TO GO

HEAVY SOULS ARE SAD ONES
BUT THEY COME BY NOW AND THEN
MAYBE GOD CAN RECYCLE THEM
AND START NEW ALL AGAIN

GOD'S LITTLE TRICK
by
Joseph Fram

GOD PLAYED A LITTLE TRICK
ON A PRIEST IN CHURCH TODAY
I THINK HE ONLY DID IT
TO SEE WHAT THE PRIEST WOULD SAY

WHEN THE PRIEST BEGAN TO TALK
HIS MIC MADE A FUNNY NOISE
THE TRICK THAT WAS BEING PLAYED
WAS TESTING THAT PRIEST'S POISE

ONE COULD SEE THE PRIEST'S ANNOYANCE
AS HE ROUGHLY SET IT DOWN
THOUGH HE DIDN'T THROW THE MIC AWAY
THERE WAS QUITE VISUALLY A FROWN

I COULDN'T HELP BUT CHUCKLE
AT THE SIGHT THAT I DID SEE
FOR I HAD TALKED WITH GOD THAT MORN
"LET'S HAVE SOME FUN," HE SAID TO ME

GOD DOES NOT MEAN US ANY HARM
HE WILL PLAY A TRICK OR TWO
HE HOPES THAT WE LAUGH WITH HIM
BECAUSE HE'S FRIENDS WITH ME AND YOU

WINDSTORM

by

Joseph Fram

SOMETIMES I SEE A WINDSTORM
BLOWING ACROSS MY MIND
IMAGES OF THE LIFE I LIVED
SWIRL SO FAST IT MAKES ME BLIND

I SEE FRAGMENTS OF MY CHILDHOOD
THERE IS PAIN AND LAUGHTER TOO
WHEN I REACH OUT TO TOUCH THEM
TOO SUDDENLY THEY ARE THROUGH

I SEE TIMES WHEN I HAD POWER
AND I KNEW THAT I WAS STRONG
THEN THE WINDSTORM TAKES THE IMAGE
I CAN'T KEEP IT VERY LONG

THROUGH THE DUST I SEE A FAMILY
TORN APART FOR WHO KNOWS WHY
AS I REACH OUT TO GRAB THE PIECES
ONLY DUST GETS IN MY EYE

AS THE WINDSTORMS COME AND GO
I JUST TRY TO UNDERSTAND
WHICH PARTS I PUT INTO MY MIND
AND THOSE IN WHICH I HAD NO HAND

WITHOUT WORDS
by
Joseph Fram

EACH TIME I THINK OF YOU
I AM LOST TO ALL AROUND
IN AM IN THAT MAGIC LAND
WHERE ONLY LOVE IS FOUND

WITH YOUR TOUCH UPON MY SKIN
HEAVEN MAKES MY BEING GLOW
HOW I LAND IN PARADISE
I GUESS I WILL NEVER KNOW

CHOIRS OF ANGELS SING TO ME
WHEN YOU TELL ME "I LOVE YOU"
THEN THERE IS PERFECT HARMONY
WHEN I SAY I LOVE YOU TOO

WHEN I SEE YOUR LOVELIT EYES
YOU MELT MY CARES AWAY
I CANNOT RESIST YOUR SMILE
WITHOUT WORDS YOU BID ME STAY

WHEN YOU TAKE ME IN YOUR ARMS
I KNOW WE WILL NEVER PART
AND EVERY KISS BECOMES A ROSE
BETWEEN THE PAGES OF MY HEART

SANDY'S SIXTY-FIVE
by
Joseph Fram

OH! SANDY, SANDY, SANDY
PERPETUAL ENERGY ALWAYS LATE
BUT YOU WON'T BE TARDY
ON THIS YOUR BIRTH DATE

YOU HAVE ZIGGED AND ZAGGED
AND KEPT US ALL ALIVE
BUT DON'T SLOW DOWN NOW
JUST CAUSE YOU'RE SIXTY-FIVE

YOU KNOW EVERYONE LOVES YOU
NOW YOU TAKE CENTER STAGE
YOU CAN GET SENIOR DISCOUNTS
WITHOUT BENDING YOUR AGE

SOME PEOPLE HAVE QUESTIONED
THEY SAY IT'S NOT FAIR
HOW YOU MANAGED TO GET HERE
WITHOUT ANY GRAY HAIR

WELL, HAPPY, HAPPY
AND MANY, MANY MORE
WE CELEBRATE YOUR BIRTHDAY
WHAT THE HECK ARE FRIENDS FOR

YOURS TO KEEP

by

Joseph Fram

I FELT YOUR ARMS AROUND ME
AND YOU NEVER SAID A WORD
LAST NIGHT WHEN I WAS ASLEEP
UNSPOKEN WORDS OF LOVE I HEARD

I FELT YOUR LIPS UPON MY NECK
AND SAW YOUR SMILE IN MY MIND
I'D LIKE TO TELL YOU HOW I FEEL
WERE SAID WITH WORDS YOU COULDN'T FIND

I AM SO GLAD I FOUND YOU
AND THAT YOU HAD NOT CHOSEN ANOTHER
WHEN I PUT MY HAND ON YOURS
IT SAID I'M GLAD WE HAVE EACH OTHER

THEN YOU DRIFTED OFF TO SLEEP
IN YOUR DREAM I SAW YOU GRIN
YOU KNEW THE ARROW CUPID SHOT
HAD FINALLY LET LOVE IN

WHEN YOUR GENTLE TOUCH MEETS MINE
IF I'M AWAKE OR I'M ASLEEP
I ALWAYS HEAR UNSPOKEN WORDS
THAT SAY MY LOVE IS YOURS TO KEEP

PAT AND RICH
by
Joseph Fram

A LITTLE PAST FIFTY YEARS AGO
A GANGLY LOOKING CHICAGO LAD
WAS CALLED TO SERVE BY UNCLE SAM
AWAY FROM HOME AND FEELING SAD

HE FILLED HIS DAYS WITH DUTIES THEN
SOMEHOW COULDN'T FILL THE EMPTY NIGHTS
HE LONGED FOR HOME AND ALL HIS FRIENDS
OR SOMETHING ELSE TO MAKE IT RIGHT

AT THAT SAME TIME A CHARMING LASS
OUT OF SCHOOL AND ON HER OWN
JUST HAPPENED BY TO CROSS HIS PATH
SINCE THAT FIRST DAY HIS HEART SHE WON

WHEN THEY WERE WED FIFTY YEARS AGO
THEY KNEW NOT WHAT LIFE WOULD BRING
THROUGH UPS AND DOWNS AND LEVEL TIMES
AFTER ALL THIS TIME TRUE LOVES DOEST SING

GOD BLESS YOU ON THIS WEDDING DAY
A LOVE FOR LIFE YOU HAVE IN STORE
THERE WOULD BE PEACE UPON THIS EARTH
IF ONLY LOVE LIKE YOURS WERE MORE

CHRISTMAS LAST
by
Joseph Fram

A LONG, LONG WAIT
AND NOW IT IS HERE
THE LAST CHRISTMAS THIS CENTURY
IS UPON US THIS YEAR

SO CHRISTMAS HAS BEEN
MANY THINGS AS I'VE GROWN
FROM SANTA AND TOYS
TO GOOD CHEER I HAVE KNOWN

BUT EACH CHRISTMAS DAY
ONE QUESTION I ASK
DID I INCLUDE CHRIST CHILD'S BIRTH
IN MY CHRISTMAS LIST TASK?

FOR THE CHRIST CHILD CAME
AND WAS SENT FROM ABOVE
WITH ONE MESSAGE CLEAR
OUR NEIGHBORS TO LOVE

NOW ON HIS BIRTHDAY
I PRAY FOR MY PART
THE SECOND COMING OF CHRIST
IS HIS LOVE IN OUR HEART

WALK WITH JESUS
by
Joseph Fram

WHEN I WALKED WITHOUT JESUS
I WAS LOST DAY BY DAY
I HAD NOTHING THAT MATTERED
AND VERY LITTLE TO SAY

I HAD FORSAKEN MY CHILDHOOD
SUCCUMBED TO THE WAY OF THE LOST
ACQUIRING ALL THING MATERIAL
AND MY SOUL WAS THE COST

GOD WATCHED ME FROM HEAVEN
BLINDLY GROPING FOR LOVE
KNOWING FULL WELL
IT MUST BE SENT FROM ABOVE

HE TOOK ALL MY POSSESSIONS
MY HOME AND MY WIFE
BUT HE DID RESURRECT ME
SO I COULD SHARE IN HIS LIFE

NOW I KNOW WHAT WAS MISSING
FROM MY LIFE ALL THOSE YEARS
MY WALK WITH SWEET JESUS
AS MY JOURNEY'S END NEARS

Coming soon!

Volume 2 of Joseph's Journey!

Reserve your copy now!

Additional copies of Joseph's Journey, Volume 1 and advance orders for Volume 2 can be ordered by sending your name and address with a check or money order for $7.95 + $2.95 shipping & handling (total = $10.90) made payable to:

Everlasting Publishing
P.O. Box 1061
Yakima, WA 98907

www.ingramcontent.com/pod-product-compliance
Lightning Source LLC
Chambersburg PA
CBHW060949050426
42337CB00052B/2941